Holy Ghost Key

Holy Ghost Key

by

Joshua Myers

BROADSIDE LOTUS PRESS
Detroit

Broadside Lotus Press

Publishers since 1965

Copyright 2024   Joshua Myers

First Edition

Printed in the United States of America

Naomi Long Madgett Poetry Award Series Editor: Gloria A. House

Photographs by Joshua Myers

Cover Art by Zal U. Ibaorimi

Book Layout: Leisia Duskin

ISBN 978-0-940713-31-4

BROADSIDE LOTUS PRESS

Post Office 02011

Detroit, Michigan 48202

www.BroadsideLotusPress.org

CONTENTS

WHOLY HOLY

WATER

GENEALOGIES

SPACES

HEALING (N'KISI)

NOTES

ACKNOWLEDGMENTS

Give praise and thanks to the musicians who offered their gifts, their vulnerabilities, their lives. To the Afro-Christian and Islamic faith communities of South Carolina, Georgia, the egbes of the Eastern seaboard, and the African histories that made them possible. To Black institutional and associational life. To grandmas on the front porch waiting out the storm. To granddads tending their own gardens. To the Savannah cohort of the Together Retreat: Ananda Lo, Anyabwile Love, Wanjiku Mwangi, and Malik J. Washington. To the earliest readers of this manuscript: Shauna Morgan, Ava Tiye Kinsey, A.B. Spellman, and Bedour Alagraa. To the whole Watering Hole tribe. And my workshop partners Franny Choi, India Hackle, Maurisa Li-A-Ping, Maria Picone and, E.J. Stephens, for their close readings. Give praise and thanks for the lives of Amiri Baraka, Sterling A. Brown, Greg Kimathi Carr, Jacob H. Carruthers, Jr, Nikky Finney, Vincent Harding, Nathaniel Mackey, Vertamae Smart-Grosvenor, Cedric J. Robinson, Sterling Stuckey, Dana A. Williams, Sherley Anne Williams, and Sylvia Wynter. To Gloria House (Aneb Kgositsile) for seeing with sharp eyes and an open heart. And Zalika U. Ibaorimi for their artistic memory.

Finally, to those who pray for liberation.

PREFACE

Sound is radical. It plunges us to the depths of feelin,[1] it takes us out to the limits, it pushes us to consider what we did not previously know. Sound is poetic. It resists categorization. Like Black people.

These are poems heard with music. In music. Alongside music. Black musics. Each poem is a returning, participating in the play of a musician or a band that I heard and have not stopped hearing since. This return is like call-and-response, like accompaniment. The dates included with each poem indicate when I first heard those sounds live. They are markers of moments where time collapsed into sound. We lost track of time and opened ourselves up to something rooted in soils deeper than mere performance.

These artists have created something larger than market relations, larger than consumer choices. They feel this music differently than those who promote and sell it. Like them, I want to write what I hear—and have it listened to. Not as ekphrasis, but as an invitation. A way to be together. A way to love.

Joshua Myers
Silver Spring, Maryland
July 15, 2023

WHOLY HOLY

"We proclaim love, our salvation."
-Marvin Gaye, "Wholy Holy"

HOLY GHOST KEY
Cory Henry
5.17.20

"I'm gon' be in B♭ all day, the Holy Ghost key!"

B♭ and still and know that I am god
      of our weary years and silent tears.
      peace be still
      help is on the way
      new mercies we seek, prayers we answer
      –ourselves.

B♭ and curve and bend notes and sounds of blackness we know
      what can wash away
      this ill.
      nothin' but the blood,
      nothin' but our blood,
      we spilled for the transubstantiation of this thing
called   the modern world.

B♭ and re-member what he's done for me oh happy day
      when precious memories linger
      long enough to erase the painful lies we already forgot.
      when we are the ghosts,
      the price of the disaster.[2]

B♭ and be holy and be acceptable unto you who be
      creating rhythms for mcintosh county shouters
      who dance blessings, offerings they summon
      right now, oh right now.
      get up and dance for these ghosts
      who refuse, with the sharp end of Ogun's hatchet.

Bb and play Hammond B-3 black whispers in the darkness
secret passages
  through mountains we can tunnel through.
  a light unto our path

  to *kalunga* lines,
  where we meet holy ghosts
  where life on the otherside is life again.

Bb and feel, for I can feel him in my soul, for I can feel him in this so
  when I reach out and touch somebody's hand.
  since all ghosts have partners, doubles,
  who practice collective escape, who be moving together.
  one and three and one and three and
  to the beat of the *djembe*
  to the kit, the tom and crash
  ride us, sweet chariot
  so that we know when we feel it,
  when spirit move through us,
  when dem bass lines move through us.

Bb and clear out these woods, and turn down the pot, only a half-step,
  a lil lower in the register where pain sat for a long time,
  for such a time as this.
  when you hum, the devil don't know what you talkin' bout.
  the hum is for us, for our ears, for our freedom
  god's gonna trouble de water,
  so says de Holy Ghost.

Bb and let that Holy Ghost key tarry, let it simmer and cook
down some,
  listen to Cory repeat the voices he heard.
  listen to life coming back around and around.

it is well
it is well
it *is well*
  with our soul....

ANTHONY HAMILTON'S SOUTHERN STUFF
Lizz Wright
10.8.21

you got that

amazing grace pentatonic
dusty dirt road drivin
one-room church house
no instrument havin
long-meter everybody harmonizin
Georgia, Alabama, Mississippi-bred
West African-rooted
Detroit, Chicago deposited
bare fingers in the grease
White Lily drop biscuit
Sunday morning dinner preppin
put something in your stomach
because pastor finna preach all day
swayin, hummin, hoopin
cuz we ain't come here for no show
Mahalia Jackson echoin
Robert Johnson sellin
front porch watermelon eatin
field pea shellin
thunderstorm watchin
sweet honey in the rock
moss tea drinkin
crab fishin
blues sweet feelin
South Carolina peach pickin
cobbler bakin
Texas sound, rock and roll worship
gris-gris carryin
swift transition fillin
muggy summer nighttime revival

clear sky gazin
lightning bug catchin
hole in the wall
fish with the bones fryin
lightbread wit mustard sandwich servin
pepsi cola mixed with somethin extra
grace givin
look the other way
law breakin
high priestess of tryon listenin

churchical frenzy
organ riffin
Ray Charles seein
choir anniversary singin
you yet holdin on
homegoing repass
soul clap, spirit doublin
freedom lovin, freedom livin
willing ourselves to
keep on keep'n on den baby

southern stuff I like

STILL PRAISE

Joel Ross
7.17.20

how we know
      though trouble assail us
      to still *praise in the midst of the storm?*

how we know
      to let everything that hath breath…
      even when they tried to
      stop our breathing
      stop our Ghosts
      stop them from inhabiting the worlds we made

where
      the sound of
      the trumpet,
      the psaltery and harp,
      the timbrel and dance,
      the stringed instruments,
      the organs,
      and

where
      cymbals crashed the place with
      the march down the aisle praise
      the gospel quartet two-step praise
      the Mississippi-blues rhythm praise.

where
        we flood this unholy place
        with praise from the fruit of our lips
        declared the haunting of Divine retribution,
        the promise of a new day, where all will see
        the God(s) in us 'fore it's everlasting too late.

where
        praises go up and blessings come down
        is not expectation
        of a transactional give and take,
        of favor ain't fair, theological malpractice,
        but a promise that God is just,
        and Holy Ghosts come back.

where
        we collectively exhale
        and we loudly exclaim
        that we believe
        what cannot be seen
        yet.

how we knew
        we knew
        that we know
        what we know
        what we know

how we knew
        to still ourselves
        to steel ourselves,
        knowing what we know.
        and knowing what we know?
        we still praise *in the midst of the storm.*

ON HOLINESS, LOVE, AND GANGSTER SHIT
Terrace Martin's Gray Area
1.11.20

Just in case anyone doubts that Black musics are holy,
let me tell you about that time Terrace Martin's Gray Area
used Blessed Assurance as the foundation for Kirk Franklin's
Love as the foundation for understanding
the ways Black folk in the Crenshaw District of Los Angeles
create community to sustain life.

L.A. gangster shit,
a survival system
for a people constantly at war with the police.

Street code,
a response
to a war that declares your existence is criminal.

L.A. is where a saxophone can save your life.

A saved life sounds like
what Nipsey Hussle's voice sounds like.
A Holy Ghost mounts Terrace Martin's horn
plays a South Central tone poem
calling for peace.

Blues for Crenshaw District warriors battling on
day in and day out,
these hard bop narrations of getting here from there.
Blues for lives lived under the I-10,
places reduced to the reductionist logic of the hood,
where there are "no humans involved."[3]

L.A. is where you encounter Valdez, dancing under the freeway.

Who reminds us that holy instruments
shape the mood of a people
who know that this thing we call life
means more than this life lived under the freeway.

Funk and soul, this sound as
foundation of the magic that pimps a butterfly.
This genealogy of struggle's persistent refrain:
live life on our terms.
Crenshaw Ghosts play the sound of Black life lived.

L.A. is where sacred music makes us whole.

Hip Hop insists on community
in the face of episodic challenges.
Crenshaw is a village,
a place to nurture a special kind of love.
Making music here is a holy task,
causing a shift, breaking something, recreating us.
It requires a deep sense of care.

L.A. is where Terrace Martin is this sound's caretaker.

Constructing altars that showcase the power of this sound,
making sure our ancestors are fed,
so we too are fed.
Listening for them,
their sound is all the evidence we need,
that folk of the Crenshaw District
have mastered how to love,
how to behold each other.

Just in case you doubted,
this is holy ground.

GOD MADE ELECTRONS, TOO
Eric Harland
4.29.21

old folk used to believe instruments plugged into electronic sockets
wasn't appropriate in the house of God
they said
electricity invited the devil that came from the juke joints.

or maybe the elders just knew that
sound was so powerful, so big
that it could blow the new roof
off the church and the building fund
committee wasn't havin' that.

or maybe–hear me out
–just maybe, *devil*
is a label that don't really capture our concept for
thinking about
how holy spirit show up in juke
joints—and the jazz jam,
(which, by the way, used to be called "devil music"
too. (footnote)
maybe devil music is just a killin' groove.

and maybe what happens in the house party
and dancehall shack ain't really a threat to the Creator,
maybe it's not evil, or wrong.
maybe it should cause y'all to question the binary of
good and evil, godly and worldly.
especially if God is
supposed to be everywhere.

after all,
Diz and Monk
and Mary Lou
heard God
and played the holy spirit in jazz clubs.

after all,
electronic sounds helped Miles
say something new,
and can't nobody tell
me that wasn't in Divine order.

after all,
Sango is said to be the orisa of electric power,
and if you ask some of us,
Jesus Christ is simply another orisa,
divine energy of Obatala.

you mean to tell me
you cannot understand salvation
and feel the spirit
through a lead guitar?

every time I feel the
Rhodes, synths, vocoder, key bass, and everything
else moving in my soul
it's a Holy Ghost good time.

when Eric Harland fill this place with Herbie Hancock
and afrobeat electronic space traveling grooves,
you're bound to notice that
there is a sweet, sweet spirit in this place.

and can't nobody tell me that ain't
the spirit of the same Lord
that made us shout

and two-step in the club last night.

WATER

"Give me water, baby, or leave me dry.
Any way you want it, I won't ask why."
-John Forte and Valerie June, "Give Me Water"

SO, REAP
Ambrose Akinmusire
8.5.18

the sounds that announce the reaping are

perhaps a haunting melody
reminiscent of a film score
made to align with a narrative of peace
offered as the sacrifice of brute force—
muscle memories
hard labor
that bring sustenance
from seeds reaped as *origami harvest*[4]

perhaps they are anticipation
of the tide coming in
making us move
altering our plans

       we do not want
       to be overcome by waters
       that might drown us

       we do want
       to be overcome by rivers
       that wash away
       memories of shame

       of having been infected
       by those who embrace the absurd conditions
       that define Black life

perhaps these sounds are like
fresh water
that might renew us
fresh air that
might help us finally
       breathe on our own

13

or maybe those sounds
are like the smell of rain coming
telling us it is time to
move inside,
get under the tent
out there is not safe

        we did not build this order
        but we will end it

these sounds will sow the ground
anticipate the flooding of the river
that will carry the resistance forth

the avant-garde
not the advance guard
not vanguard

the trumpet bars
key bass lines
hurtling through
this morass
this Hell

compositions that anticipate
what peace feels like
sounds like
to our Black lives

this sound is an announcement
a break beat
and it declares
you will have to
reap with us
love us – or not
for we will love ourselves
because we out here
really out here

contorted, but not torn
this *origami harvest* is here.

FAITH
Robert Glasper
12.4.18

Truth sounds less dense than the sea, made of that substance, that make buoys, that make life vests, that make rafts, that make canoes, that make the oars the ferryman use to rescue us, to rescue a people cast adrift in the ocean, swallowed up in the wake of the sinking, stinking ship that tries to drown our faith, but can't. our faith is the substance of things Anna Julia Cooper hoped for. she said: faith means treating the truth as true.[5]

This substance made the sound coming from these piano keys, gave it confidence, a firmness, possessed it with reassurance, and a boom bap, hip hop love song, swinging to the beat of the faith of our fathers, our mothers. Sprinkle some in this bag, spread it around your house, in the hallways, the door cracks, clean your counter with it, shine your pots with it, dry your clothes with it, leave a little in your pillowcase, so you, too, will know, really know, that everything will be everything. it will float.

PRESENCE
Tyshawn Sorey
3.29.19

The toms announce their presence, roaring through the forest,
with muffled shouts of timber, trees fall,
lumber is cut, shaped into the bows of boats
that secret the worries away. Secrete the words
of those making their escape plans known only to the few.
We feel the presence of rhythms that shape our
journeys through thickets, swamps, rivers,
and paddle away in our boats, as thunderclaps and lightning
bolts spark
explosions of percussion,
a storm of cover.

Through the clearing, where Baby Suggs said love
our presence, we get stuck in mud made by last
night's rain. Don't sink, let rhythm dig
our feet out the mirey clay, so we will be ready when
the wind beckons us, makes
its presence known to us. We move under
a canopy of trees, the bird's singing
announcing their presence, softly covering our tracks
across broken branches,
our limbs aching from the pain.

Singing work songs makes our journey feel shorter through
the forest, across the river, into the clearing, through the canopy
and toward the big lake. We work the songs
into the pain, massage it out, tell it to
study war no more. The rhythm calms us.

Soon will we make it to the big lake,
the open water, where we know there is a presence,
where it all began. We will march to the edge, come close,
feel her presence. We will feel our way to a transition,
a renewed presence in the form of this vibration,
an eternal pulse that sustains, that goes on,
that makes us listen.

RESIDENCE TIME
Eric Harland
11.19.20

submerged in moods,
baptized under modal
forces, underwater
aquatic journeys
to restart the residence time of
life cycles that join life
force with the flow of
the deep sea; the ocean
floor welcomed ancestors
who relived lost cities
of Atlantis, whose movement
and rhythm
drove a frenetic
energy, drove the improvisational
pull into the water's
mood, the plunge
breaking down the sonar,
alerting those
meant to rescue dem
thought lost, dem who
have found
residence
in the water's time.

Ambrose Akinmusire Quartet, City Winery,
Washington, DC, September 22, 2022

HOW SEA CALL
Ambrose Akinmusire
9.22.22

summon the tide to send us over
into this deep blues
register, where the meanings of
Hyacinth's love for his people
meant an embrace of a portal that
sent him down, deeper and deeper
down here below, where the trumpeter makes sound
into heavy, sustained measures,
sure of their relation to life, sure of their relation
to what death cannot kill.

out here where the sea is calm, undisturbed
by order's antagonism, order's opposition
to Black life lived along rhythms,
along waves, where a kick drum
propels us through the water's expanse;
rhythms that are plans for life,
plans against sinking into the depths of social relations
that announce us dead on arrival.

out here, in and under the water,
they cannot hear us
cannot feel us;
this vibration is ours, made in relation to those
who know Yemanya's call,
her soothing, nourishing, nurturing summoning,
possessed by
tunes made to invite those seeking safe passage
to life lived differently.

this underworld is what Sylvia Wynter meant
by the under-life[6], the underlying rhythm
of tom-toms, riding currents
that are pointed exclamations
of living histories–
organisms for the remaking of us,
heretofore unmarked, uncategorized
and named only by an ancestral
libation that is performed out here
in this oceanic hush harbor
safe in the arms of those who chose the water.

still, they cry for us.
crying is a signal for connection, for touch–
crying is a calling out of those in need,
and they need us,
they need to be remembered
they need us to feed them, to feel them,
they need us to see them,
to finally reconnect our lives to theirs,
so their living was not be in vain,
so our living will not be in vain.

the tone of this piano tells us of
these healing waters,
an ocean of memory calling us to *weheme mesu*.[7]
these sound waves and vibrational currents
are hydrotherapy, taking us out
from here to there to somewhere else,
somewhere
other than where the sea last brought us.

GENEALOGIES

Genealogy and lineage don't matter within jazz and who's
who and what's what is based primarily on the corporate
and critical establishments.
–Nicholas Payton, "Black American Music
and the Jazz Tradition"

Being present begins with an awareness of
one's immediate genealogy.
–Greg Kimathi Carr, "Inscribing African World History"

THE LOOP IS HISTORY
Nicholas Payton
6.11.20

the *djelis* met in Congo Square every week, trading notes, sharing sounds, exchanging their country marks, to record patterns, chart new ways of addressing what was and is this unprecedented mess we find ourselves in.

they met over and over, and meetings became dance, and dance became language, became the Blues, became dooo duuhhhh dooooo, the story of we, #BAM[8], an ancestral birthright to get it together.

the story repeats the message, the message is the music, the story is this music, funk and groove on a loop, the loop is the heartbeat of we, #BAM, an imperative to let no one take what is ours.

we are born into the repetition, and we do not die, we only transition, we loop the beat; but we still gotta make sure we sit down together–and plan.

we still gotta meet to make sure we never let this circle be broken.

FLAME CARRYING
Jason Moran and the Bandwagon
7.31.22

you said "nobody start a fire like Geri Allen,"
and nobody tend flames like the bandwagon,
working that rhythmic kindling, keeping the tradition alight.
the bandwagon rides through like a flaming chariot,
coming forth to carry us, spirit us home.

Thelonious fire, Waller fire, it keep spreading,
then the left hand booms.
an eruption.
damn, how that happen?
how you sneak dynamite on stage?

blasts around the bass lines, we now encased
in all this heat, burning fast.
now slow,
black people love a 350 degrees oven
warming us, like the Harlem 369th.
James Reese Europe warmed us,
warned us, that fighting in hell
meant fighting Great Wars over there and at
home.

Negro music is the Great War,
a reimagination of ragtime,
recognizing the African roots of war.
Hellfighters hellfighting meant we return fire,
we return fighting.[9]
A symphonic march scorches earth, slashes and burns
this concept of home (of the brave).

REPEAT THE BIRTH
Ben Williams + Marcus Gilmore
10.16.20

it is possible for two
hearts to beat in
sync, to create
the pocket with acoustic
stringed rhythms, perfectly
narrating the courage
and litheness
it takes to strip our melodies
down to the bottom, where the
Blackest haints are
finding beautiful ones
lying in wait, anticipating the day
they will be born again.

all that is possible.

BLUE IS THE COLOR OF THE SHADOW
Robert Glasper + Chris Dave + Derrick Hodge
1.27.18

relive hip hop blues that
take shelter within shadows
of ancestors, shaped into the curve
      of A Love Supreme.
linger with the sound a little while,
to cast a shadow a little while,
maybe dance, maybe hope,
definitely pray a little while.

listen as rivers of blue passages
flow into port cities, spreading along coasts,
extending as an extended lyr(e)ic, strings riffin' like
Nathaniel Mackey signifyin' on
sixteen bars, sixteenth notes semiquaver,
sixteen Black ministers meeting to declare
desires for families, to till blue fields
protected and remade as collective harvest,
honest work on lands available to all who need a place

pray that their children remember
the ways the blues wrap their heads
around grapevines of great clouds of witnesses,
that their children tend their resting places
with blue roses, planted along the fields
where each generation dreamed of their own
forty acres of blue chords,
tugging and pulling, playing bass lines,
making the bass line up
      the melody of Afro Blue
which is the word
passed, heard in their rememory.[10]

blue bottle flies offer melodic crosspollination,
a sonic organic chemistry that makes
          children Fall in Love.
this ain't a sad blues, it's hip hop tinted,
tinctured like the Blues first made with
hands dyed like Julie Dash's vision of
the past.[11]
like the Peazants, young children will hold
the ancestors close, and wait a little while,
because something is coming, a suspended
drum roll launches patient reflection into
radical expectation.
and that's the blues,
whether indigo colored or haint paint.
with see-through waters
that ripple with the wind,
shadows spill grief and loss, re-sounded
as another beginning.

James Francies, The Blue Note, New York, October 25, 2021

RHYTHM-A-NING
James Francies + Joel Ross + Mike Mitchell
10.25.21

to lose a name is certain death.

      melodies haunt
      freedmen's towns in Houston
      given an inheritance
      by working people
      all across the landscape of islands
      tributaries and mountaintops, playing in
      red hill churchyard,[12] clapping to the rhythms
      of the lives and struggles of Negro
      toilers, who learned them from ancient
      Bluespeople whose vibraphone and key bass
      had other names like *balagon* and *kongoma*
      creative sound as our eternal reflection

so we would not die.

sometimes I can hear those old masters,
see their wry smiles
their looks of approval
laughing because somehow their
children's
      children's children's children's children's children's
children
still know a rhythm they played–
not their names not their language,
but this syncopation.

names unknown reappear through
death portals in the sound that brings

      the chill
      the *whew*
      the tears.

this rhythm is a libation,
a rekindled ancestral fire

making their names
        show up and break open a drumstick or mallet
        burdened with carrying thousands
        of years of memory

they show up
to tell us that freedom is in the rhythm

living is playing rhythm-a-ning

if you ain't hear that, the fire alarm was for you.

MARCH DANCE SHADOWS

Marcus Gilmore
1.29.21

bakongo soldiers marched
and high-stepped through swampland
parading and drumming
along the Stono River[13], in lands
devoted to evil, with hands delivering
fatal blows to evil. these soldiers danced
with the devil. displaced the devil's
claim to forbearance, the devil's system of
belief. the march was a dance, the
drum was a call, a beckoning to all
who could hear that sound
that made revenge less a fantasy
than a radical break,
less a happy ending, than
a destination where one could contemplate
how a cymbal could ride.

a cymbal of life as a sustained declaration
of how to live in difference,
indifferent to
everything but the sounds that march
to the beat of a different drummer, this drummer.
let them embrace you
like a long-delayed first meeting,
where two or three feets are gathered together,
and sounds make shadows in the midst,
make them use shade,
and take cover to pray silently in the mist,
in the small rain, *medupe*[14]
for a people beholden to
a different belief system in
relation to this world,
as the only way to
march down this road,
dance the way the soldiers did.

camped around their fire,
their shrieks were heard in the distance
where emancipation
was only a proclamation of a shout made
for us, by us.

listen for cymbals,
for a symbol that signifies
sincere belief in utopic measures.
that is how it feels when
the march of different time signatures
erupts order and
old soldiers hold on and
march to beautiful, beautiful Zion.
dancing here, praying here,
where they chose to live.

FREE[1]
James Brandon Lewis
11.20.21

free
   1.

      this little word be causing all kinda ruckus.

      marauding, colonizing, enslavers made
      "free" Africans in North Carolina wear
      FREE on they arms.

      made them different from
      those who skin bored the names of free men
      who said they was building democracy.

      needed words on they arm
      to remind them of their status needed to read
      FREE to mute the meaning of their skin.

      wanted to keep them under control,
      keep them separate from their "property,"
      keep their slavery safe in the bosom of their "democracy."

      kicked "free" Africans out of the state,
      made them cross that "strange river in Canaan,"
      lest they confuse things further.

      sent them to a place not much different,
      where you had to be vigilant
      for police, and the feds too.

      a place where they asked:
      what it mean to be free
      in a land where three million people were your
      hereditary bondsmen?

2.

this little word be imagination

looking out, holding on,
the African's society for mutual relief,
mutuality as being held together.

a ceremony,
an emancipation day parade,
a glory, glory hallelujah.

Frederick Augustus Washington Bailey marrying
Anna Murray soon as he got clear of the South,
becoming Douglass.

a flight to the hinterlands,
a shotgun blast, if necessary,
stowing in the hold of a ship.

stride piano,
this insistence and gesture of
non-capturable rhythm.

let J.P. Johnson fingers tell it,
they liberal democracy couldn't define our
stride toward freedom.

they history lie and pretended
we only wanted to be
good Americans the whole time.

ancestors broke away,
turned over in they graves
at feeble attempts to make us sing patriotic songs.

3.

this little word be shouting out.

ancestors crying out,
because we still
ain't free.

the Blues ain't no negotiation
with the Devil,
Robert Johnson was really talking to Esu.

they way wasn't it,
and these Blues can't win you no Grammy,
these Blues are ante-political: non-ownable.

if a political project,
if an art-making philosophy,
these Blues transcended political reality.

you can't vote for the Blues,
and it can't betray you,
even when you try to capture like the Lomaxes.

James Brandon Lewis rides this freedom train,
felt as a lullaby
and a hush.

4.

this little word is a whisper.

tell the music critics and dissertation writers
to just...
hush.

for somebody's calling our names
somebody's making us
feel again.

reach out and touch this musical land,
renewed spaces of the free,
these ancestors, who renewed the land with free sound.

hush…
stop thinking so hard,
be free.

this music frees the land,
breaks up the soil,
displacing a history of suffering.

this little word
offers a haunting meditation
for ancestors who need avenging.

FREE$_2$

James Brandon Lewis
11.20.21

free
    5.

        to live in Gwendolyn Brooks's
        belief in
        the along[15]

        relief,
        fresh air along the
        meeting of two oceans

        good hope for a good life
        in this along,
        settling down feels like a warm embrace

        hugs that last an extra beat,
        sitting up under each other
        real lazy like–

        a Sunday afternoon,
        napping into the evening
        that never transitions into Monday

        that feeling stays there in the along
        along this way, where
        everyday will be like Sunday

        after while–
        these will all be *soulful days*
        in the along

we will not
welcome the-end-of-the-song
in the dominion

of listening for each other
matching the rhythms
of our heartbeats

and telling stories of what
we missed when we weren't allowed
to live here

allowing ourselves space
for worrying, strands of sound
meant to stitch our lives together

cold nights
wrapped together in the warmth
of the along

rent apart,
only to be placed back together as
quilts of new imaginations

cold nights held together
by blues
on the corner

hold me in the along
take me to the water
let this night air

meet me where the seashore begins
let the water remind
me where freedom moves along

BIRTH OF THE COOL
Terrace Martin's Curly
10.9.22

some major league pitchers throw easy gas,
their minimal effort masking technical mastery.
we just call that
          cool.

real cool don't need no marketing plan.
sit at their feet, listen to paths tread through
ancestral musical force.
let it be what it
          is.

no pretense necessary.
play what comes to you,
make that make do, make it be
          enough.

create sweetness out of a radical hope,
a fervent prayer,
that really makes us
          believe.

in life:
a brew of disparate elements, an organic chemistry,
cooked slowly,
spirits mixed and mastered for
          us.

make the Hammond B3 carry this mystery,
not for articulate doctrine,
but a life more sweeter, a life real
          cool.

SPACES

...land is space, territory, on which people can begin to
reconstruct their lives....
–Robin D.G. Kelley, Freedom Dreams

Living as I have argued we do in the wake of slavery, in spaces
where we were never meant to survive, or have been punished for
surviving and for daring to claim or make spaces of something
like freedom, we yet reimagine and transform spaces for and
practices of an ethics of care (as in repair, maintenance,
attention), an ethics of seeing, and of being in the wake
as consciousness...
–Christina Sharpe, In the Wake

Space is the place.
–Sun Ra

Kamasi Washington, Sixth and I Synagogue,
Washington, DC, June 7, 2022

OUT OF SPACE
Kamasi Washington
6.7.22

o u t
names the sound of betrayed expectation,
launches a vibration to sentient beings who call
space home. an invocation that shows earthbeings
their theories of everything are inconsequential in
the grand scheme
of the
u n i v e r s e.

p a r a d o x:
a sound so large that it tells
us to acknowledge
our smallness. an enactment of Truth that
deflates our ego, and listens for something greater
than the self.
not a paradox:
c l a r i t y.

SPACE/ ACCOMPANIMENT
Robert Glasper
4.12.19

Space as silence arranged for spirit, felt and heard. Resonant without feeling, silenced there to be felt some other time. In another time.

> Space as occupation, or for being occupied. For taking up. For leaving.

Space as connection with other dimensions   of ourselves.

> Space as the meaning of passage, passing along. Never withholding, sharing here and there.

> Space as accompaniment for the self, playing the changes, worrying the line, hearing the self, so the self can hear others.

> Space as accompaniment for spirit. Accompaniment for the groove. Groove for spirit.

> Space as preparation for improvisation with the self.

> With each other.

We enter arm in arm. We catch ourselves. We say little. We groove for each other.

Space as a memorial for the living. Accompaniment for living together, being honest with one another. Accompaniment is loving together love's opening.

Space as the thing that never forgets to be silent.

That time, that opening, that call, that   love.

NOTES ON KINETIC
James Francies
2.15.19

I.

distant, infinite destinations
travels in space, journeys in outer space
these notes on kinetic launched a
North Star-following, drinking gourd intellectual genealogy
around the Sphere
of Thelonious, who said I mean you,
and he really do. *Dobale.*[16]
With these notes we mean to
offer spaces to open, a re-opening
to a blues people blueprint,
a plan and a map where the infinite destination is
space for exploring the debt and depth we owe
to ancestors who declared a war against death.

these notes on kinetic created spaces
for sound solemnity, structured sedimentation.
ground broken up,
blues notes planted deeply in fresh soil,
a way of seeing and sowing what makes us whole.
these notes, resonant powerful progressions,
where fingers leap and sway, swinging and chopping,
evoking emotional gravity, elegying euphonic grace.
you will realize
these notes on kinetic are electric blues, charged-up,
activated spaces for dreaming, again and again,
that continuity, ceaseless stream of consciousness is
resolution, not order.

II.

out of primeval "nothingness," came everything
"nothing music" is never just nothing[17]–
Nun is darkness, void, space.
this sound is dark purple,
vibrant and royal, herald of creation.
space for prophetic restatements
of swing time. miles ahead of Nardis,
our legendary lineage, our unbroken chain
ties us to a space to re-member.
even as we make new territory,
we are buoyed by ancestral re-imagination.
these notes on kinetic are
straight chops,
enigmatic, ethereal restatements.
not a monument, not construction, not a state.
space is Nun.[18]

everything required for creation was always there.
sound is a mirror of that fullness,
smoothed and rounded,
completing cycles.
creation as music's ritual practice, round and round.

music's deliberate, emphatic journey around the sun
toward the view from the bridge,
where we can again see resolution,
observe change. like Monks,
we inhale the Evidence.

these notes on kinetic reveal tone and color,
spectral space-time,
painted harmony, panoramic rhythm
melody given as speech, the making of all things.

space is not *this* place.
return us to space as cycle, as relation, as movement.
return us to
space as Ptah satisfied, the repetition of creation,
or just beginning again.

constant movement,
kinetic energy,

sounds that start the world over.

Chief Xian aTunde Adjuah and R+R=Now, The Blue Note,
New York, November 28, 2018

FOR NINA
R+R=*NOW*
11.28.18

Nina calls.
they reflect and respond to
these times.

that time
Robert Glasper's graceful piano lines and
keyboard passages responded to
Terrace Martin vocoding,
wading in water, responding to

   butterflies spread across blue skies

   autumn nights at the blue note

found Chief Xian's rich
dark hues responding to
Derrick Hodge and his
ritual healing bass, responding to
Justin Tyson's sonorous,
rumbling drum kit, responding to
a Taylor McFerrin booming
beatbox beat machine,

   sounding off riffing on each other.

Robert's band of brothers respond to
each other, but also respond to
us, who need each other,

   who need these brothers to

build sound for safe passage
to spaces for renewal and healing,
for care and attention.

spaces to stop and consider
each other
and what we can build
together.
spaces for artists to
say what it is about now

that must   change.

they make sound   make transformation.

and if you ain't hear all that,
at least you heard
Justin's chops,
Terrace's tone,
Chief's phrasing,
the depth,
of Taylor's colors in the dark.

you   at least fell into

Derrick's crater of emotion,
imploding from center stage,
straight into our hearts,
Nicole Hurst sing to our hearts.
sing forever in our hearts.

Nina   we will reflect the time.

we will heed the time.
believe it's time
to tell ourselves that
we ain't goin' back,
we stayin' in this space,

this   space.

Immanuel Wilkins Quartet, Newport Jazz Festival,
Newport, RI, July 31, 2021

FLIGHT PLAN
Immanuel Wilkins
7.31.21

In the beginning we said let there be flight

we moved away from these valleys
we moved away from these fields
into the respite of mountains
fortified by breastworks of spirit
we moved

Immanuel Wilkins is retracing their steps
hearing them, hear him

calling

calling

calling

us all the way off the ground
to the height of the treetops
soaring like Sugarman

listen

listen

listen

to this playing
it is rememory
breathless transportation
it is submission to Divine force

surrender

surrender

surrender

to this horn's air
breathe it in
surrender them tears,
ride them
and know you will be cared for
when you arrive
no more sorrow song

Immanuel Wilkins is showing us how to get up in
an upper room in this house with no walls

In the beginning there was the word that told us to escape
and there was this sound

WE MADE INSTRUMENT
Chief Xian aTunde Adjuah
11.22.2021

After Ashon Crawley

Whose breathing move silences
      through instruments, brass instruments
         made to announce war.

The creation of Diaspora,
      a blunt instrument.
      Enslavement,
         an instrument of death.

Black peoples, Black sounds, Black spirits
      who use instruments, made instruments.

      We remade those instruments of
      murder.

To tell us of ourselves   To sound new meanings
To craft new imaginations

Who used these same instruments,
      who made new instruments,
         whose breathing moved silences.

Who re-imagined that these instruments can
be made instrument,
can be signposts announcing
liberation,
      rather than maafa.

Whose new instruments of ancestral recall,
      made instrument, stringed instruments,
      to carry our memory,
      like blood throughout the body.

Kora, carrier of the weight of a people's past
      strung together, made instrument.
      New instruments connected our sound, stretched music
          to yesterday,
            which is today and tomorrow.
                Time is stretched across the bow.

Stringed instruments, made instrument to disrupt
      oceans that could have obstructed our memory, but did not.
      Cora's son made instrument, made an instrument,
      combining *kora* and *kamele n'goni,*
      designed to let fingers breathe, like digital *djeli,*
      a made instrument as re-evaluation.

Palms of our hands on skins that were made instrument,
      stretched on the stumps of trees, hollowed out to recall
      ancestors, who will be made instrument,

To tell stories   To tell us what must be re-evaluated
To tell us of a space

Of regeneration
Djembe and *conga* made instrument
      to carry rhythm and displace pain.

DREAMSCAPES
Jason Moran and Robert Glasper
4.16.22

like a dreamscape,
breath returns

to us as love,
packaged as sound.

to have lived in these sounds is
to have been tickled by this spirit,

to have been touched in a way,
that disrupted anything that arrested us;

to have been heard
and felt,

to have glimpsed the kind of world we could have,
if sound had its way.

it was only a moment,
but if you were there, you

would know what it was to feel
the dreamscape.

to feel feelings
unfettered by protocols of power and control,

to release the desire
for things figured out, all measured, and precise.

with sound returned to us as breath,
we can free words from an impossible burden.

this love-giving, sound gathering,
is about a different way

of being in concert, perfect in its ability
to take us somewhere

ephemeral, escaping the clutches of the world
that says it cannot be.

sound, breath— these dreamscapes, this love.

SING TO RE-MEMBER
Somi
4.21.21

what can we know of who we are *in the absence of things?*

stripped bare
left with nothing
denuded
placeless
our bodies exhumed into exile

reduced to
       breath
       blood
       muscles

what do we dream about *in the absence of things?*

of home
       a Dakar compound where drum, kora, and guitar
       conspire with Abbey Lincoln's scream
       her saut,
       us moving together 'round the Kaaba,

a place where you knew *you could always touch your feet
to the floor*

to market days
full of expectations
spectators in vibrant colors
ankara-draped streets
where birds echo the chatter,
their music punctuating the air

a whisper, a hiss, an exhale,
then a yell, a wisdom instruction:
don't forget to breathe

catching our breath
       does not fill the absence;
       the void is there
       as marker of space
       it is where we stop to consider
       what we have when we have nothing

our voices
whisper and hiss and yell:
I, who have nothing,
we who have nothing
       have something(s) after all

the songs are our holy room
Allahu Akbar

the trees sway in response
we thank them,
use their bodies
to craft tools to mirror our voice,
       the first instrument

don't forget to breathe
repeats her mother's instructions,
for there is never truly absence
unless we forget to sing

HEALING (N'KISI)

"*N'kisi*[19] of the root-verb *kînsa* ("to take care"), is what takes care of life…it can either be safe or dangerous to the owner and the user."
– Kimbwandénde Kia Bunseku Fu-Kiau,
Self-Healing Power and Therapy

COME OUT
Immanuel Wilkins
3.27.21

submit to sound as invocation of Blues blood sacrifice. sound
as offering to the spirits, placed in large kettles over fire, vittles
piled high on plates, placed under oak trees, buried underneath
the ground, provision for blessings. the alto saxophone builds
a shrine to a ritual for a Black future. ancestors, come on out,
come out. the blood run deep, vocal lines run deep, invoking
safe passage for gods who need space to sit as they negotiate
on our behalf. sing in memory of those who gave blood, not as
nostalgia, but as a mercy. this Blues blood is a mercy. and we
are everything. we are everything we need. chant their names,
sing their praises. these phrases are for their ease, for their
comfort. sweet melodies, haunting rhythms show us what we
been through, what we leave behind, what is promised us. the
blues have sentenced us to time served. come out. the Blues
blood has blessed the land, has blessed my family. these musi-
cian-diviners have made the sacrifice.

HEALING
Esperanza Spalding
7.30.22

the Haitians say Francois Mackandal turned into
a little fly.
a little spirit visited on those who could not believe
we possessed something they could not see.
life force
arrangements against the machines.
for when you dream you possess a desire to be well,
and we were sure we wanted to be well.

we made formwelas[20], spells to cast out
the demon spirits who wrested power and authority
from charisma, imprisoned us in
political systems, knowing nothing about
how we could sing this illness on out.

because *sound is really a thing.*

minor key minor complexes
mind her, mine the half-steps.
hearing is a labor.
hearing is liberation,
like seeing.
like opening whole passages,
allowing
wild roots *firm in the ground*
to guide whole notes, operatic lines, hold notes,
held out for us, whole hosts
phrasing holy ghosts.
their
love is like the wind.
Wild–that hearing it is
like healing.

Georgia Anne Muldrow + Nyeusi, The Sandlot,
Washington, DC, June 8, 2019

REMINDED OF THE GOOD THINGS
Georgia Anne Muldrow + Nyeusi
6.8.19

they bring her shadows
  she shapes them into language
  decoding African deep thought as a
sacred insurrection, political resonance
  for struggle as a dance of unity.

they bring her dulcet tones, rhythmic gesture
  she offers vulnerability, she addresses
  tension, pressure as possibility. she pounds
  the fibers of fruits, that carry seeds
  of the people's memory, that carry
  lessons for how life can be remade.

they bring her roses and lay them at her feet
  she walks through their imagination,
  slicing through alienation, inviting
  to ceremony, fomenting rebellion
  made through chords stitched together,
  they are *reminded of the good things.*

they bring her bars
  she erects structures, spaces as
  monuments to the Blues, the funk
  as salve against chaos, reordering
  structures, planting and blooming
  houses of love.

they bring her groove
  she listens to the Nyeusi beat, presses
  her heart against theirs, summons the wind
  to carry them through.

they bring her to the edge
  she looks over, asks them to trust her,
   to believe they can make it down. she says:
  "before I'll be a slave, I'll be buried
  in my grave."

and they swing.

THE OTHER SIDE OF THE BREAK
Joel Ross
2.26.21

played in a time where everything known as
comfort is taken away, making room for something new.
what's new is what Avey Johnson[21] must have felt
as she was escorted heart-to-heart by the sacred energy
that transforms us on the other side of the break.
that's what these vibes feel like: well-being. being so welled up
in an emotion you don't want to release because
you fear gravity will push you back down into the depths
that sound made you escape. take off your shoes for you are on the
holy ground of cascading arpeggios, a creative-improvised
spiritual bath illuminating tones that root out unnoticed harm.
notice this is a spirit-filling station on a long journey.
dance the highs the lows the ins and outs. inhale each solo, each
sustained quarter note given to you for safekeeping.
a song as the warrant of an experience prayed over as a parting gift.
cross this bridge and you'll find that you have been blessed with a
soundtrack to gettin' over, pressing on as reverberation.
it is a reminder to be steel. you can play it anytime you want.

CHARM SCHOOL
Amythyst Kiah
10.22.22

I.

these guitars played
like charms, amulets
gris-gris instruments
as protection from the
pain of broken circles
and lapsed memories
of how to play,
which Dizzy said
is a form of worship.

these guitars clear
paths, clean glasses
of water held underneath
mattresses offering
second sight for a people
washed away.
for the people who
were whisked away.

these guitars, broken bottles
shattered glasses for
acoustic linkages
to times and places
where dusty roads
and shallow ponds
mark territories, new maps
for finding God revealed
in the troubles of the world.

II.

her voice is a lake house,
warmth-filled cabin,
the smoke of a doused
outdoor hearth, permeating
the senses, anticipating
the utter relief of sustenance
that is coming.
that must come.

her voice is a holy
inheritance given as
our common will,
the guitar strings, its executor.
to make sure we
experience care, she sings for us,
she sings for
old-time ancestors.

her voice insists on
the possibility of resolution
of our common terror
and our minor key pain.
it can be called out and
measured and examined,
can be known and diagnosed.
      the blues are our secret code
      for knowing our healing
      is imminent.

III.

these guitars,
her voice
invoke time as common experience,
history as living through
rhythms that never stop,
passages of time sound
the same
      and different.

these guitars,
her voice
face the world
and confront sadness, despair
joy, and the melodic fullness of hope.
they are the ordinary registers
of life, frailty
and strength, angst and wonder,
a blues mood.

these guitars,
her voice
offer relief in extraordinary times,
times of trouble, intermediary periods,
maafa[22]

these guitars,
her voice
offer *minkisi*
>against capitalist modernity
>and the colonization of time, memory
>against the idea of a neoliberal order
>that declares there is no alternative.

these guitars,
her voice are
sound as charm,
harmony that
replaces harm,
takes harm back
to its proper place.
but there is a river,
Blacksounds are sculls of memory.

these guitars,
her voice,
rhythmic divination,
vocal conjuration,
are holy implements
of love.

WANNA GO THERE

Chris Dave and the Drumhedz + STOUT
5.28.2022

after Paule Marshall

an invitation arrives in the form of rhythm, an accent, an emphasis driven by the r in R&B. it says follow me here, follow the cadence to release the thing that bound you, restricted you. rhythm is the key to unleashing, releasing, to feeling, being whole.

it says to meet your guide under the cover of night, a location deep in the delta blues fields, too dark to see with your eyes, yet dark enough to behold sounds of meditation, sustained echoes of voices whispering like owls telling the stories that make campfires sites of potent memory.

it says in the morning you will experience liberation – but you must first experience the nighttime sounds of darkness passing through where the guide will sing to you, will offer vibration and noise, will tell you of the day her heart quivered, her mind surrendered to this neo-soul awakening new soul gospel journey. the day she got souled out selling out concerts with audiences of all souls, saints gone marching in, who are now gathering, awaiting the moment of your arrival.

the guide's meditative voice pierces the depth of blue-black expanse and widens the aperture of shadowy shapes appearing as heralds of something ominous.

she says trust her. she sings like a strong wind. this is a ritual that requires vulnerability and open-ness. she sings the invitation again: wanna go there? and you say: "Of course, I'm going…"[23]

she listens, nods and then sings you to sleep. a warm lullaby offers calm, respite, a mother's peace, a grandmother's prayer.

and then morning comes. the guide no longer uses words. melodic utterances, scats scatter the debris of the night. a hum and moan register improvisation, open up space and groove. you say you *wanna go there.*

she moans and you follow.
the gravelly path turns into a
winding road.

it seems endless.

it goes for miles

and miles.

twigs and branches are strewn
along the way, piled along the
side of the road bordered by
thousands of trees. the scent
of pine, birch, and oak arrests
you.

the trees disappear, give way to a clearing, the road straightens. a single ancient baobab appears. the path encircles this landmark. the road honors its anteriority.

the guide asks you to go around it. and you wind around this life cycle, to see what awaited beyond the *kalunga.* a field of goldenrods, then lilies, which were a direction. the guide sings to them and you follow her. you walk alongside flowers planted at the foothills to welcome you.

you look up, climb the hill, where there is a large revival tent. there you hear people, a low hum, then a drumbeat, another rhythm. it feels traditional, it feels new.

they spill out of the tent. women wearing white dresses, accented with blue and gold. men wearing white linen, accented with red and purple. they greet you, they smile, they ask you if you are ready.

the guide disappears as
the men and women take you
by the arm into the tent.
the drums continue.
     the escorts dance.
         you lose yourself.
            you follow them.
               you sway and moan.
                  and sing and hum.

you learn the
words
immediately.
even though
you do not
know their
meaning, they
are familiar.

hours pass and you feel no ways tired. the beat goes on. and soon it begins to slow. the eldest of the group makes their way through the men and the women to reach you. staring into your eyes, the elder asks: "And who you is?"[24]

        a new beat emerges furiously.
        the peace is broken, a spell cast.

then they come, clad in gold, wearing long dresses, wrapped tightly, bounded with grace, concealing something too precious to reveal to undeserving eyes. adorned with gold jewelry and headbands affixed with figurines, goddesses reposed on long braids arranged in tufts – these twenty women whom the elder and drums summoned.

> they march up the hill in rhythm and take you to a small shack close by. you enter trembling, but not fearful, for you have never experienced love in this way. they mark your head with ritual blood, an offering to remind you that everything has a cost. liberation is what we are willing to sacrifice.

they tell you of their journey, and you find their story familiar. you ask them how they managed to escape and what their lives are now. and you ask them how they found you. they say your body "might be in Tatem," but we always knew "your mind was long gone with the Ibos."[25]   you had to be ready for their invitation.

they took you so that they could give you
>> their goddesses,
>> and your ancestors,
>> your birthright
>>> and your *ori*.[26]

so that they could cleanse you
of the thing that you thought
was going to make you whole.

> these twenty women made you well
> they released you.

you return to the tent
all is calm
no more dancing
the ritual has ended.

a priest says:
to all gathered, a job well done.

you look around and those who
once danced are sitting together,
embracing and holding each other,
offering expressions of love and
tenderness. they are not tired, they
seem satisfied. dusk approaches
announcing the demise of the day,
and they turn to you as if to say: "…
You's all right now, oui…you must
tell me you's all right?"[27]

and you are grateful for the invitation.

Notes

1 Bettina Judd, Feelin: *Creative Practice, Pleasure, and Black Feminist Thought* (Evanston: Northwestern University Press, 2022).

2 These stanzas echo W.E.B. Du Bois, *Black Reconstruction in America*, 1860-1880 (New York: Free Press, 2000).

3 Sylvia Wynter, "No Humans Involved: A Note to My Colleagues," *Forum NHI* 1 (Fall 1994): 42-71.

4 This is the title of Akinmusire's 2018 project.

5 Anna Julia Cooper, A *Voice from the South: By a Black Woman of the South* (Xenia, OH: Aldine, 1892), 300.

6 A reference to Sylvia Wynter's *Black Metamorphosis: New Natives in the New World*, forthcoming.

7 *Weheme mesu* is a Middle Egyptian term which means "the repetition of the birth." See my *Of Black Study* (London: Pluto Press, 2023), 134-38, for other references.

8 #BAM is Black American Music, a movement started by Nicholas Payton to rethink the meaning of our musical heritage and displace the genre-specific labels affixed to it.

9 W.E.B. Du Bois, "The African Roots of War," *Atlantic Monthly* (May 1915): 708-14; W.E.B. Du Bois, "Returning Soldiers," *The Crisis* (May 1919): 13-14.

10 From Toni Morrison's novel, *Beloved*. In an recently unearthed essay, Morrison writes her sense of the word: "History versus memory, and memory versus memorylessness. Rememory as in recollecting and remembering as in reassembling the members of the body, the family, the population of the past." Morrison, "Rememory" in *The Source of Self-Regard* (New York: Alfred A. Knopf, 2019), 324.

11 *Daughters of the Dust*, dir. Julie Dash (1991).

12 References to Red Hill Churchyard, as well as many of the other ancestral rituals, flow from this collection's engagement with the work of Sterling Stuckey, whose primary argument is that the ring shout and African cultural and spiritual practices form the basis for African American identity and political unities, what some have also called our fictive kinship and linked fate. See Sterling Stuckey, *Slave Culture: Nationalism and the Foundations of Black America* (New York: Oxford University Press, 1987).

13 During the 1739 Stono Rebellion in Stono, South Carolina, enslaved Africans were said to have marched across plantations to the sound of their own drums.

14 *Medupe* is a Tswana word meaning "small, drizzling, rain." In Ayi Kwei Armah's *The Eloquence of the Scribes*, there is this offering of its meaning: They called their troupe *Medupe*. I asked what the word meant. "Small rain," Malesa Lebelo said, before Dumakude ka Ndlovu added that farmers where they lived distinguished between two types of rain. One type was violent, spectacular, pouring down tremendous torrents in a short period, sweeping away topsoil, uprooting fragile vegetation, causing erosion, making gullies and ravines. Big, useless rain. Small rain, on the other hand, fell slowly, so softly it felt like mist. Lasting hours and days on end, it could moisten soil for planting, and irrigate growing crops without damaging land. It was the kind of rain that did the groundwork for future harvests. The children from Soweto wanted their poetry to do that kind of patient, slow, long-term, practically invisible preparatory work." *The Eloquence of the Scribes* (Popenguine, Senegal: Per Ankh, 2006), 125.

15 Gwendolyn Brooks, "Speech to the Young," https://poetrysociety.org/poetry-in-motion/speech-to-the-young-speech-to-the-progress-toward-among-them-nora-and-henry-iii.

16 A Yoruba word, translating roughly as "show of respect."

17 "In this playing of "nothing," it is not that nothing is played, that nothing is heard; it is that what appears is the sound of the gift of unconcealment." Ashon Crawley, *Blackpentecostal Breath: The Aesthetics of Possibility* (New York: Fordham University Press, 2016), 258.

18 *Nun* is a Kemetic deity/concept meaning primeval waters and often translated as nothingness; but as Jacob Carruthers has shown, this uncreated existence is not merely "nothing." See his *Mdw Ntr: A Historiographical Reflection of African Deep Thought from the Time of the Pharaohs to the Present* (London: Karnak House, 1995), 32-33.

19 The terms *"nkisi"* and *"minkisi"* are Bakongo terms that can be translated roughly as sacred medicine. These were often physical implements and concoctions used to ensure maximal health and solve disease related problems. They are one of the many bases of hoodoo practices among Africans in the New World. See among others, Michael Gomez, *Exchanging Our Country Marks: The Transformation of African Identities in the Colonial and Antebellum South* (Chapel Hill, NC: University of North Carolina Press, 1998), 275.

20 The "formwela" is a sonic invention of Esperanza Spalding and the Songwrights Apothecary Lab, meant to promote healing and wellness. A collection of these may be found in the 2021 album, *Songwrights Apothecary Lab.*

21 Avey Johnson is the central character in Paule Marshall's, *Praisesong for the Widow* (New York: Putnam, 1983).

22 *Maafa* is Kiswahili for "great disaster," and is often used to describe the long history of enslavement and colonialism experienced by Africans and their lineages across the modern world.

23 Paule Marshall, *Praisesong for the Widow* (New York: Putnam, 1983), 229.

24 Ibid, 251.

25 Ibid, 255.

26 *Ori* is the Yoruba concept of "destiny."

27 Marshall, *Praiseong,* 229.

ABOUT THE AUTHOR

Joshua Myers, PhD, is the author of three books and multiple articles on African American culture and politics. He is Associate Professor of African American Studies at Howard University. His poems have appeared in *Obsidian: Literature and Arts in the African Diaspora*, and in the anthology, *Doors*, Burning House Press, December, 2018.

ABOUT THE ARTIST

Zal U. Ibaorimi, PhD, is an undisciplinary artist and Assistant Professor of Gender and Women's Studies at the University of Illinois, Urbana-Champaign.

THE NAOMI LONG MADGETT POETRY AWARD

Dr. Naomi Long Madgett, nationally celebrated poet and publisher of Lotus Press, established the Naomi Long Madgett Poetry Award in 1993, with the mission of recognizing and publishing outstanding African American poets. Since the merger of Lotus Press and Broadside Press in 2015, Broadside Lotus Press has continued the annual project. African American poets may submit original, unpublished manuscripts of at least 50 pages in length in March of each year. All submissions are reviewed by the Award Series Editor at Broadside Lotus Press, with a nationally recognized, distinguished poet naming the final winner. The winning poet receives a monetary award, and Broadside Lotus Press publishes the manuscript in the following year.